THE FIFTH DAY

The Fifth Day

EDITED BY MARY Q. STEELE

DECORATIONS BY JANINA DOMANSKA

GREENWILLOW BOOKS

A DIVISION OF
WILLIAM MORROW & COMPANY, INC.
NEW YORK

Library of Congress
Cataloging in Publication Data
Main entry under title: The Fifth day.
Summary: An anthology of nature poems
by English and American poets.
1. Nature—Juvenile poetry.
2. Children's poetry, American.
3. Children's poetry, English.
[1. Nature—Poetry.
2. American poetry—Collections.
3. English poetry—Collections.]
I. Steele, Mary Q.   II. Domanska, Janina.
PN6110.C4F49   821'.008'036
77-26143   ISBN 0-688-80146-3
ISBN 0-688-84146-5 lib. bdg.

For Ada,
with love and thanks

INTRODUCTION

I have always liked poetry. For many years I
have wanted to make, simply for myself, a book
containing all the poems I like best. But when
I stopped to consider, I realized that such a book
would be too large to go on any shelf. It
would be enormous.

Because I am a sort of naturalist I have sometimes thought I would compile for other people
a volume of poems concerned with nature,
with trees and foxes and birds and crickets and
weather. But once again I discovered that there
would be too many poems I could not bear
to omit from such a collection.

Now that I have in fact edited an anthology, I
have limited myself to poems concerned with
all those things which were present on this
planet at the end of the fifth day of creation:
"And God said, Let the waters bring forth
abundantly the moving creature that has life,
and fowls that may fly above the earth in the
open firmament of heaven.

"And God created great whales, and every
living creature that moveth, which the waters
brought forth abundantly, after their kind, and
every winged fowl after his kind: and God
saw that it was good.

"And God blessed them, saying be fruitful
and multiply, and fill the waters in the seas, and
let fowl multiply in the earth."

I have interpreted this passage to mean all living
creatures below the order of mammals. I have
excepted whales, which we think to be mammals,
though who knows? When God created them
he may first have devised them as fish, as now we
are learning that dinosaurs were not lizards
and that the descendants of those marvelous
beasts are not crocodiles lazing in the mud of
the Nile but the sweet-voiced woodthrush
singing on our doorsteps.

Flowers and mountains and tides and seasons
were present then too, and I have included some
poems about these. And one mammal *is*
ever-present, that sad small sixth-day postscript,
humankind. For poets are men and women,
and without their powers of observation and
their talents I could have offered you no book
at all.

I have used only English and American poets
for English is the only language I read with any
ease and I was fearful of translations. And I
have discovered that fewer poets than I at first

supposed were interested in the creatures I
had selected for my subject matter. Only birds
seemed to have a really wide appeal and even
the birds were more apt to be swans and
nightingales than sparrows and nuthatches.
Up until fairly recently poets were most often
content to use snakes and eagles as symbols
of evil or nobility. Perhaps they were too closely
associated with the lower forms of life to
regard them with much curiosity. The kind of
exactly descriptive lyric such as Theodore
Roethke's "The Heron" is a modern innovation
—though not so innovative at that. For by
his accurate observation of the wading bird,
Mr. Roethke like earlier poets has intended to
remind us of our own humanity and what we do
and do not have in common with other forms
of life.

No one of us can know what the world was truly
like at the end of the fifth day. For that reason
I have begun with a poem by Shelley which has
always, unaccountably, conjured up for me a
sense of how it might have felt to be present
when the world was just beginning, and I
have ended with a poem by Conrad Aiken which
pictures what sadly earth may become again.
The others have been arranged in no special

order, only in a way that pleased me and seemed to give a pleasant texture to the whole.

I hope that you will like some of these poems, that you will want to read more poems like them and by some of the same authors. But beyond that I hope they will cause you to look more closely and more kindly at some of the humble and occasionally despised inhabitants of earth, those things God gazed upon and saw that they were good.

Mary Q. Steele

CONTENTS

xi

THE FIFTH DAY

THE WORLD WANDERERS

Tell me, thou star, whose wings of light
Speed thee in thy fiery flight,
In what cavern of the night
    Will thy pinions close now?

Tell me, moon, thou pale and gray
Pilgrim of heaven's homeless way,
In what depth of night or day
    Seekest thou repose now?

Weary wind, who wanderest
Like the world's rejected guest,
Hast thou still some secret nest
    On the tree or billow?

                    Percy Bysshe Shelley

THE WOOD FROG

I came across my cousin,
sunning itself, and I presumed
on kinship with a touch. Like leaves,
joined in their camouflage with fox
and squirrel, an autumn russet,
it was a pulse of earth on earth;
with white neck fluttering, black eyes
steeper than lake water, black waters.
Then it let me pick it up
and put it down again—
so still and self-sufficient,
so far from me,
I gave up all presumption.

John Hay

THE DOOR

One in the boat cried out
Pointing to land,
For the sun leaped clear of the mist
And a rainbow spanned
With one vast arch the mountain, the trees and
   the sand.

The mountain stood like a huge
Ghost in a cloud;
The startled trees were caught
In a wavering crowd;
And the four in their glittering oilskins cried
   aloud

As that pure and soaring arch
More marvelous grew,
And the sandhills stared beneath it
Wild and new,
And down the unearthly beaches lamenting flew

Gull upon gull distraught
Blown through that Door,
Handful on handful flung
High over the shore.
Such desperate beauty they never had seen before.

L. A. G. Strong

LEAVES

Peace to these little broken leaves,
That strew our common ground;
That chase their tails, like silly dogs,
As they go round and round.
For though in winter boughs are bare,
Let us not once forget
Their summer glory, when these leaves
Caught the great Sun in their strong net:
And made him, in the lower air,
Tremble—no bigger than a star!

W. H. Davies

Therefore all seasons shall be sweet to thee,
Whether the summer clothe the general earth
With greenness, or the redbreast sit and sing
Betwixt the tufts of snow on the bare branch
Of mossy apple-tree, while the nigh thatch
Smokes in the sun-thaw; whether the eave-drops
    fall
Heard only in the trances of the blast,
Or if the secret ministry of frost ·
Shall hang them up in silent icicles,
Quietly shining to the quiet Moon.

Samuel Taylor Coleridge

THE WHELK

The whelk in his shell
growing too cool
crept out in the sun and lying
there as in an oven
was soon cooked and eaten whelk-whole.
It was not man nor woman
drawn from man, was without blood bone or soul
yet as kindred without shell
it stole my compassion.

Janet Frame

6

THE BOOK OF HOW

After the stars were all hung separately out
For mortal eyes to see that care to look
The one who did it sat down and wrote a book
On how he did it.
                                    It took him about
As long to write the book as to do the deed
But he said, "It's things like this we mostly need."
And the angels approved but the devils screamed
        with laughter
For they knew exactly what would follow after.

For somehow he managed entirely to omit
The most important facts in accomplishing it,

Where he got the ladder to reach the stars
And how he lighted them, especially Mars,

And what he hung them on when he got them
        there
Eternally distant and luminous in the air.

                                    Merrill Moore

NO JEWEL

No jewel from the rock
Is lovely as the dew,
Flashing with flamelike red
With sea-like blue.

No web the merchant weaves
Can rival hers—
The silk the spider spins
Across the furze.

Walter de la Mare

WHY?

The murmur of a bee
A witchcraft yieldeth me.
If any ask me why,
'Twere easier to die
Than tell.

The red upon the hill
Taketh away my will;
If anybody sneer,
Take care, for God is here,
That's all.

The breaking of the day
Addeth to my degree;
If any ask me how,
Artist, who drew me so,
Must tell!

Emily Dickinson

ROSAMUND'S SONG
FROM "BECKET"

Rainbow, stay,
Gleam upon gloom,
Bright as my dream.
Rainbow, stay!

But it passes away,
Gloom upon gleam,
Dark as my doom—
O rainbow, stay!

Alfred, Lord Tennyson

THE COFFIN-WORM
which consider

The Worm unto his love: lo, here's fresh store;
Want irks us less as men are pinched the more.
Why dost thou lag? thou pitiest the man?
Fall to, the while I teach thee what I can.
Men in their lives full solitary be:
We are their last and kindest company.
Lo, where care's claws have been! those marks
    are grim;
Go, gentle Love, erase the scar from him.
Hapless perchance in love (most men are so),
Our quaint felicity he could not know:
We and our generation shall sow love
Throughout that frame he was not master of;
Flatter his wishful beauties; in his ear
Whisper he is at last beloved here;
Sing him (and in no false and siren strain)
We will not leave him while a shred remain
On his sweet bones: then shall our labour cease,
And the imperishable part find peace
Even from love; meanwhile how blest he lies,
Love in his heart, his empty hands, his eyes.

Ruth Pitter

THE FEAR OF FLOWERS

The nodding oxeye bends before the wind,
The woodbine quakes lest boys their flowers
    should find,
And prickly dogrose spite of its array
Can't dare the blossom-seeking hand away,
While thistles wear their heavy knobs of bloom
Proud as a warhorse wears its haughty plume,
And by the roadside danger's self defies;
On commons where pined sheep and oxen lie
In ruddy pomp and ever thronging mood
It stands and spreads like danger in a wood,
And in the village street where meanest weeds
Can't stand untouched to fill their husks with
    seeds,
The haughty thistle o'er all danger towers,
In every place the very wasp of flowers.

                                    John Clare

CROCIDILES

A crocidile dont hunt
Him's victims
They hunts him
All he do is
Open he jaws

Ishmael Reed

DIRGE IN WOODS

A wind sways the pines,
          And below
Not a breath of wild air;
Still as the mosses that glow
On the flooring and over the lines
Of the roots here and there.
The pine-tree drops its dead;
They are quiet, as under the sea.
Overhead, overhead
Rushes life in a race,
As the clouds the clouds chase;
          And we go,
And we drop like the fruits of the trees,
          Even we,
          Even so.

George Meredith

LINES WRITTEN ON LEARNING THAT THE IVORY-BILLED WOODPECKER IS NOT AFTER ALL EXTINCT

Arise oh phoenix from your own ashes from your
    own dust
Upon the altar of the sun in a ball of myrrh
Sweet-smelling out of your own death arise

Oh crimson immortal bird made mortal again
Born on a funeral pyre cradled in cinders
Ascending impossibly from regions of air and
    darkness
To subsist once more upon flat-headed borers
To climb once more the trunks of dead trees
    uttering
Cries like the sounds of a child's toy trumpet . . .

Mary Q. Steele

from AN ODE TO THE RAIN

Composed before daylight, on the morning appointed
for the departure of a very worthy, but not very pleasant
visitor, whom it was feared the rain might detain.

Dear Rain! I ne'er refused to say
You're a good creature in your way,
Nay, I could write a book myself,
Would fit a parson's lower shelf,
Showing how very good you are.—
What then? sometimes it must be fair!
And if sometimes, why not to-day?
Do go, dear Rain! do go away!

And this I'll swear to you, dear Rain!
Whenever you shall come again,
Be you as dull as e'er you could
(And by the bye 'tis understood,
You're not so pleasant as you're good),
Yet, knowing well your worth and place,
I'll welcome you with cheerful face;

And though you stay'd a week or more,
Were ten times duller than before;
Yet with kind heart, and right good will,
I'll sit and listen to you still;
Nor should you go away, dear Rain!
Uninvited to remain.
But only now, for this one day,
Do go, dear Rain! do go away.

Samuel Taylor Coleridge

LINES TO A DRAGON FLY

Life (priest and poet say) is but a dream;
I wish no happier one than to be laid
Beneath a cool syringa's scented shade,
Or wavy willow, by the running stream,
Brimful of Moral, where the Dragon Fly
Wanders as careless and content as I.

Thanks for this fancy, insect king,
Of purple crest and filmy wing,
Who with indifference givest up
The water-lily's golden cup,
To come again and overlook
What I am writing in my book.
Believe me, most who read the line
Will read with hornier eyes than thine;
And yet their souls shall live for ever,
And thine drop dead into the river!
God pardon them, O insect king,
Who fancy so unjust a thing!

                    Walter Savage Landor

from AUTUMN

I heard a bird sing in the woods to-day
A failing song:
The times had caught on him!

In autumn boughs he tried a wonted lay;
And was abashed to find his music grim
As the crow's song.

Then, when I raised an air
To comfort him,
I wretched was to hear

The crow did croak
And chatter everywhere
Within my ear.

James Stephens

TO A WILD GOOSE
OVER DECOYS

O lonely trumpeter, coasting down the sky,
Like a winter leaf blown from the bur-oak tree
By whipping winds, and flapping silverly
Against the sun,—I know your lonely cry.

I know the worn wild heart that bends your flight
And circles you above this beckoning lake,
Eager of neck, to find the honking drake
Who speaks of reedy refuge for the night.

I know the sudden rapture that you fling
In answer to our friendly gander's call—
Halloo! Beware decoys!—or you will fall
With a silver bullet whistling in your wing.

Beat on your weary flight across the blue!
Beware, O traveler, of our gabbling geese!
Beware this weedy counterfeit of peace!—
Oh, I was once a passing bird like you.

Lew Sarett

THE AMBER BEAD

I saw a fly within a bead
Of amber cleanly buried:
The urn was little, but the room
More rich than Cleopatra's tomb.

Robert Herrick

A MINOR BIRD

I have wished a bird would fly away,
And not sing by my house all day;

Have clapped my hands at him from the door
When it seemed as if I could bear no more.

The fault must partly have been in me.
The bird was not to blame for his key.

And of course there must be something wrong
In wanting to silence any song.

Robert Frost

from EPISTLE TO JOHN HAMILTON REYNOLDS

Dear Reynolds! I have a mysterious tale,
And cannot speak it: the first page I read
Upon a Lampit rock of green sea-weed
Among the breakers; 'twas a quiet eve,
The rocks were silent, the wide sea did weave
An untumultuous fringe of silver foam
Along the flat brown sand; I was at home
And should have been most happy,—but I saw
Too far into the sea, where every maw
The greater on the less feeds evermore.—
But I saw too distinct into the core
Of an eternal fierce destruction,
And so from happiness I far was gone.
Still am I sick of it, and tho', to-day,
I've gathered young spring-leaves, and flowers gay
Of periwinkle and wild strawberry,
Still do I that most fierce destruction see,—
The Shark at savage prey,—the Hawk at
    pounce,—
The gentle Robin, like a Pard or Ounce,
Ravening a worm, . . .

John Keats

SPIDERS

Why does she like spiders?
Bitty as beads, fat as comfits,
Treading the air in kitchen and bathroom,
Shinning up pipes to strand themselves
In porcelain wastelands:
What's the attraction?

She argues: they have personality.
I wouldn't know,
I've never talked to one.
Each autumn they invade my house.
Cramming their eggs in corners,
Cosy as cotton-wool inside an ear.

They pay their way. Each window
Is a boneyard. What I resent
(Not on behalf of flies)
Is their stupidity. They drown
In puddles, roast in burning logs:
It's carelessness, not suicide.

And yet she grieves.
These juicy yo-yos, mithering their young
Are all her creatures.
Cats may not kill them.
Birds are given crumbs.
Careful, she says, here comes a big one.

Philip Oakes

TO AN ICICLE

Chilled into a serenity
As rigid as your pose
You linger trustingly,
But a gutter waits for you.
Your elegance does not secure
You favors with the sun.
He is not one to pity fragileness.
He thinks all cheeks should burn
And feel how tears can run.

Blanche Taylor Dickinson

FLYING CROOKED

The butterfly, a cabbage-white,
(His honest idiocy of flight)
Will never now, it is too late,
Master the art of flying straight,
Yet has—who knows so well as I?—
A just sense of how not to fly:
He lurches here and here by guess
And God and hope and hopelessness.
Even the aerobatic swift
Has not his flying-crooked gift.

Robert Graves

Of the birds that fly in the farthest sea
six are stranger than others be:
under its tumble, among the fish,
six are a marvel passing wish.

First is a hawk, exceeding great;
he dwelleth alone; he hath no mate;
his neck is wound with a yellow ring;
on his breast is the crest of a former king.

The second bird is exceeding pale,
from little head to scanty tail;
she is striped with black on either wing,
which is rose-lined, like a princely thing.

Though small the bulk of the brilliant third,
of all blue birds 'tis the bluest bird;
they fly in bands; and, seen by day,
by the side of them the sky is grey.

I mind the fifth, I forgot the fourth,
unless that it comes from the east by north.
The fifth is an orange white-billed duck;
he diveth for fish, like the god of Luck;

he hath never a foot on which to stand;
for water yields and he loves not land.
This is the end of many words
save one, concerning marvellous birds.

The great-faced dolphin is first of fish;
he is devil-eyed and devilish;
of all the fishes is he most brave,
he walks the sea like an angry wave.

The second the fishes call their lord;
himself a bow, his face is a sword;
his sword is armed with a hundred teeth,
fifty above and fifty beneath.

The third hath a scarlet suit of mail;
the fourth is naught but a feeble tail;
the fifth is a whip with a hundred strands,
and every arm hath a hundred hands.

The last strange fish is the last strange bird;
of him no sage hath ever heard,
he roams the sea in a gleaming horde
in fear of the dolphin and him of the sword.

He leaps from the sea with a silken swish;
He beats the air does the flying fish.
His eyes are round with excess of fright,
bright as the drops of his pinions' flight.

In sea and sky he hath no peace;
for the five strange fish are his enemies;
and the five strange fowls keep watch for him;
they know him well by his crystal gleam.

Oftwhiles, sir Sage, on my junk's white deck
have I seen this fish-bird come to wreck,
oftwhiles (fair deck) 'twixt bow and poop
have I seen this piteous sky-fish stoop.

Scaled bird, how his snout and gills dilate,
all quivering and roseate:
he pants in crystal and mother-of-pearl
while his body shrinks and his pinions furl.

His beauty passes like bubbles blown;
the white bright bird is a fish of stone;
the bird so fair, for its putrid sake,
is flung to the dogs in the junk's white wake.

John Gray

TILL I WENT OUT

Till I went out of doors to prove
What through my window I saw move;
To see if grass was brighter yet,
And if the stones were dark and wet;

Till I went out to see a sign—
That slanted rain, so light and fine,
Had almost settled in my mind
That I at last could see the wind.

W. H. Davies

SUMMER'S OBSEQUIES

The gentian weaves her fringes,
The maple's loom is red.
My departing blossoms
Obviate parade.

A brief, but patient illness,
An hour to prepare;
And one, below this morning,
Is where the angels are.

It was a short procession,—
The bobolink was there,
An aged bee addressed us,
And then we knelt in prayer.

We trust that she was willing,—
We ask that we may be.
Summer, sister, seraph,
Let us go with thee!

In the name of the bee
And of the butterfly
And of the breeze, amen!

Emily Dickinson

THE HERON

The heron stands in water where the swamp
Has deepened to the blackness of a pool,
Or balances with one leg on a hump
Of marsh grass heaped above a musk-rat hole.

He walks the shallow with an antic grace.
The great feet break the ridges of the sand,
The long eye notes the minnow's hiding place.
His beak is quicker than a human hand.

He jerks a frog across his bony lip,
Then points his heavy bill above the wood.
The wide wings flap but once to lift him up.
A single ripple starts from where he stood.

Theodore Roethke

THOUGH ALL THE FATES
SHOULD PROVE UNKIND

Though all the fates should prove unkind,
Leave not your native land behind.
The ship, becalmed, at length stands still;
The steed must rest beneath the hill;
But swiftly still our fortunes pace
To find us out in every place.
The vessel, though her masts be firm,
Beneath her copper bears a worm;
Around the cape, across the line,
Till fields of ice her course confine;
It matters not how smooth the breeze,
How shallow or how deep the seas,
Whether she bears Manila twine,
Or in her hold Madeira wine,
Or China teas, or Spanish hides,
In port or quarantine she rides;
Far from New England's blustering shore,
New England's worm her hulk shall bore,
And sink her in the Indian seas,
Twine, wine, and hides, and China teas.

Henry David Thoreau

from THE CICADAS

Limp hangs the leafy sky; never a breeze
Stirs, nor a foot in all this sleeping ground;
And there is silence underneath the trees—
The living silence of continuous sound.

For like inveterate remorse, like shrill
Delirium throbbing in the fevered brain,
An unseen people of cicadas fill
Night with their one harsh note, again, again.

Again, again, with what insensate zest!
What fury of persistence, hour by hour!
Filled with what devil that denies them rest,
Drunk with what source of pleasure and of power!

Life is their madness, life that all night long
Bids them to sing and sing, they know not why;
Mad cause and senseless burden of their songs;
For life commands, and Life! is all their cry.

Aldous Huxley

THE KRAKEN

Below the thunders of the upper deep,
Far, far beneath in the abysmal sea,
His ancient, dreamless, uninvaded sleep
The Kraken sleepeth: faintest sunlights flee
About his shadowy sides; above him swell
Huge sponges of millennial growth and height;
And far away into the sickly light,
From many a wondrous grot and secret cell
Unnumber'd and enormous polypi
Winnow with giant arms the slumbering green.
There hath he lain for ages, and will lie
Battening upon huge sea-worms in his sleep,
Until the latter fire shall heat the deep;
Then once by man and angels to be seen,
In roaring he shall rise and on the surface die.

Alfred, Lord Tennyson

THE ROSE FAMILY

The rose is a rose,
And was always a rose.
But the theory now goes
That the apple's a rose,
And the pear is, and so's
The plum, I suppose.
The dear only knows
What will next prove a rose.
You, of course, are a rose—
But were always a rose.

Robert Frost

DEATH AND LIFE

Apparently with no surprise
To any happy flower,
The frost beheads it at its play
In accidental power.
The blond assassin passes on,
The sun proceeds unmoved
To measure off another day
For an approving God.

Emily Dickinson

CHAMELEON

Ancient and leaden-lidded he treads
A branch's tight-rope balancing his double times
Unsteadily, a calculating creeper stirs
Something alive out of extinct tellurian dreams.

Age with blood as green as youth,
Gay as a pigmy sunset painted on a leaf,
A crouching abstract of the sky
And flower and earth, savage in arthritic grief.

Suffers the puppy's caress
Of a bounding wind, unsoftened and not yet
    undone,
Watching behind his painted walls
In a small darkness, spun on a broken axle of sun,

Juggles the two hemispheres
On the black ridge of our old dilemma, plies
His patient, palaeolithic anger
With a hissing tongue on a diet of present flies.

Anthony Delius

AN AUGUST MIDNIGHT

I

A shaded lamp and a waving blind,
And the beat of a clock from a distant floor:
On this scene enter—winged, horned, and
    spined—
A longlegs, a moth, and a dumbledore;
While 'mid my page there idly stands
A sleepy fly, that rubs its hands . . .

II

Thus meet we five, in this still place,
At this point of time, at this point in space.
—My guests besmear my new-penned line,
Or bang at the lamp and fall supine.
"God's humblest, they!" I muse. Yet why?
They know Earth-secrets that know not I.

Thomas Hardy

from THE WATER OAKS

. . . In the beginning there were three
And in the end there shall be only three:
The trees, the river,
And the outspread lonely tree of heaven,
Whose boughs are blossomy apple-wreaths at
   dawn,
Autumnal red and purple in the sunset,
And laden, night long, with the fruitage of the
   stars,
A harvest for some still-delaying husbandman.

William Alexander Percy

LARKS

All day in exquisite air
The song clomb an invisible stair,
Flight on flight, story on story,
Into the dazzling glory.

There was no bird, only a singing,
Up in the glory, climbing and ringing,
Like a small golden cloud at even,
Trembling 'twixt earth and heaven.

I saw no staircase winding, winding,
Up in the dazzle, sapphire and blinding,
Yet round by round, in exquisite air,
The song went up the stair.

Katherine Tynan Hinkson

THE SOLES

The soles are lying in shallows off Dungeness
   Spit.
They rest on vacant sides and stare at the sun.
Their skin like sand is glowing against the sand.

The tide has come and gone. It comes again.
The soles are lying still as their own breath.
The ocean passes through the straits of their gills.

One eye has moved an inch in a million years
To join the other on the burning side,
Drawn up like a moon from underlying night.

They dart and bury themselves as we drift over.
They cloud the sand across their speckled halves.
Their fixed, their wandering eyes stare up again.

                        David Wagoner

INVERSNAID

This darksome burn, horseback brown,
His rollrock highroad roaring down,
In coop and in comb the fleece of his foam
Flutes and low to the lake falls home.

A windpuff-bonnet of fawn-froth
Turns and twindles over the broth
Of a pool so pitchblack, fell-frowning,
It rounds and rounds Despair to drowning.

Degged with dew, dappled with dew
Are the groins of the braes that the brook treads
   through,
Wiry heathpacks, flitches of fern,
And the beadbonny ash that sits over the burn.

What would the world be, once bereft
Of wet and of wildness? Let them be left,
O let them be left, wildness and wet;
Long live the weeds and the wilderness yet.

Gerard Manley Hopkins

WATER-FOWL

Mark how the feathered tenants of the flood,
With grace of motion that might scarcely seem
Inferior to angelical, prolong
Their curious pastime! shaping in mid air
(And sometimes with ambitious wing that soars
High as the level of the mountain-tops)
A circuit ampler than the lake beneath—
Their own domain; but ever, while intent
On tracing and retracing that large round,
Their jubilant activity evolves
Hundreds of curves and circlets, to and fro,
Upward and downward, progress intricate
Yet unperplexed, as if one spirit swayed
Their indefatigable flight. 'Tis done—
Ten times, or more, I fancied it had ceased;
But lo! the vanished company again
Ascending; they approach—I hear their wings,
Faint, faint at first; and then an eager sound,
Past in a moment—and as faint again!

They tempt the sun to sport amid their plumes;
They tempt the water, or the gleaming ice,
To show them a fair image; 'tis themselves,
Their own fair forms, upon the glimmering plain,
Painted more soft and fair as they descend
Almost to touch;—then up again aloft,
Up with a sally and a flash of speed,
As if they scorned both resting-place and rest!

William Wordsworth

SNAKE

I saw a young snake glide
Out of the mottled shade
And hang, limp on a stone:
A thin mouth, and a tongue
Stayed, in the still air.

It turned; it drew away;
Its shadow bent in half;
It quickened and was gone.

I felt my slow blood warm.
I longed to be that thing,
The pure, sensuous form.

And I may be, some time.

Theodore Roethke

THE WOODSPURGE

The wind flapped loose, the wind was still,
Shaken out dead from tree and hill:
I had walked on at the wind's will,—
I sat now, for the wind was still.

Between my knees my forehead was,—
My lips, drawn in, said not Alas!
My hair was over in the grass,
My naked ears heard the day pass.

My eyes, wide open, had the run
Of some ten weeds to fix upon;
Among those few, out of the sun,
The woodspurge flowered, three cups in one.

From perfect grief there need not be
Wisdom or even memory:
One thing then learnt remains to me,—
The woodspurge has a cup of three.

Dante Gabriel Rossetti

THE MAYFLY

Love me but once I say,
For once sufficeth;
I sink at close of day,
The next one riseth.
Behold me where I go,
Lost if you stay me not;
I am a breath, and so
Love and delay me not.

Some splashing undergrad
Engulfs my neighbour;
Yon greedy trout hath had
Ten with no labour.
A speedy death I see
Below and above me,
The only remedy
Is that you love me.

I the day's beauty am
And the night's sorrow
From the dark deep I came
And go to-morrow.
Love me while yet I shine
In my best feather,
And for grief's anodyne
We'll die together.

Ruth Pitter

POST IMPRESSIONS

III

the wind is a Lady with
bright slender eyes(who

moves)at sunset
and who—touches—the
hills without any reason

(i have spoken with this
indubitable and green person "Are
You the wind?" "Yes" "why do you touch flowers
as if they were unalive, as

if They were ideas?" "because, sir
things which in my mind blossom will
stumble beneath a clumsiest disguise, appear
capable of fragility and indecision

—do not suppose these
without any reason and otherwise
roses and mountains
different from the i am who wanders

imminently across the renewed world"
to me said the) wind being A lady in a green
dress, who; touches: the fields
(at sunset)

                                        E. E. Cummings

VESPERS

O blackbird, what a boy you are!
How you do go it!
Blowing your bugle to that one sweet star—
How you do blow it!
And does she hear you, blackbird boy, so far?
Or is it wasted breath?
"Good Lord! she is so bright
To-night!"
The blackbird saith.

Thomas Edward Brown

THE BLINDED BIRD

So zestfully canst thou sing?
And all this indignity,
With God's consent, on thee!
Blinded ere yet a-wing
By the red-hot needle thou,
I stand and wonder how
So zestfully thou canst sing!

Resenting not such wrong,
Thy grievous pain forgot,
Eternal dark thy lot,
Groping thy whole life long,
After that stab of fire;
Enjailed in pitiless wire;
Resenting not such wrong!

Who hath charity? This bird.
Who suffereth long and is kind,
Is not provoked, though blind
And alive ensepulchred?
Who hopeth, endureth all things?
Who thinketh no evil, but sings?
Who is divine? This bird.

Thomas Hardy

FOUR SNAKES

Four snakes
Gliding up and down a hollow
For no purpose that I could see—
Not to eat, not for love,
But only gliding.

Ralph Waldo Emerson
Lines from his Journal
arranged by Mary Q. Steele

from WOOD, AN INSECT

. . . an insect they call a Wood Louse,
That folds up itself in itself for a house
As round as a Ball, without head, without tail,
Inclos'd *Cap-a-pee* in a strong Coat of Mail . . .

Jonathan Swift

THE SNOWFLAKE

Before I melt,
Come, look at me!
This lovely icy filigree!
Of a great forest
In one night
I make a wilderness
Of white:
By skyey cold
Of crystals made,
All softly, on
Your finger laid,
I pause, that you
My beauty see:
Breathe, and I vanish
Instantly.

Walter de la Mare

from MEDITATIONS OF
AN OLD WOMAN

As when silt drifts and sifts down through muddy
pond-water,
Settling in small beads around weeds and sunken
branches,
And one crab, tentative, hunches himself before
moving along the bottom,
Grotesque, awkward, his extended eyes looking
at nothing in particular,
Only a few bubbles loosening from the ill-matched
tentacles,
The tail and smaller legs slipping and sliding
slowly backward—
So the spirit tries for another life,
Another way and place in which to continue;
Or a salmon, tired, moving up a shallow stream,
Nudges into a back-eddy, a sandy inlet,
Bumping against sticks and bottom-stones, then
swinging
Around, back into the tiny maincurrent, the rush
of brownish-white water,
Still swimming forward—
So, I suppose, the spirit journeys.

Theodore Roethke

TO THE GRASSHOPPER
AND THE CRICKET

Green little vaulter in the sunny grass
Catching your heart up at the feel of June,
Sole voice that's heard amidst the lazy noon,
When ev'n the bees lag at the summoning brass;
And you, warm little housekeeper, who class
With those who think the candles come too soon,
Loving the fire, and with your tricksome tune
Nick the glad silent moments as they pass;
Oh sweet and tiny cousins, that belong,
One to the fields,the other to the hearth,
Both have your sunshine; both though small are
    strong
At your clear hearts; and both were sent on earth
To sing in thoughtful ears this natural song—
In doors and out, summer and winter, Mirth.

James Leigh Hunt

SNAILS AND SLUGS:
A DISTINCTION

Snails
Climb up their stairs,
Look out their doors
To test the weather.

Slugs,
On the other hand,
Never go inside—
Rain, heat, or snow—
Have no doors to peer from,
Slide down no banisters.

Mary Q. Steele

A FRAGMENT

Wake the serpent not—lest he
Should not know the way to go;
Let him crawl which yet lies sleeping
Through the deep grass of the meadow!
Not a bee shall hear him creeping,
Not a May-fly shall awaken,
From its cradling blue-bell shaken,
Not the starlight as he's sliding
Through the grass with silent gliding.

Percy Bysshe Shelley

from SUNRISE

... my gossip, the owl—is it thou
That out of the leaves of the low-hanging bough,
As I pass to the beach, art stirred?
Dumb woods, have ye uttered a bird?

Sidney Lanier

There is nothing moving there, in that desert of
    silence,
Nothing living there, not even a blade of grass.
The morning there is as silent as the evening,
The nights and days with an equal horror pass.

Nothing moving except the cold, slow shadow
Thrown on sand by a boulder, or by the cliff
Whose rock not even a lichen comes to cover,
To hide—from what?—time's ancient hieroglyph.

The sun, at noon, sings like a flaming cymbal
Above that waste: but the waste makes no reply.
In all that desolation of rock and gravel
There is no water, no answer to the sky.

Sometimes, perhaps, from other lands more
    happy,
A faint wind, slow, exhausted, ventures there,
And loses itself in silence, like a music.
And then—who knows?—beneath that alien air,

Which moves mysteriously as memory over
Forlorn abysms and peaks of stone and sand,
Ghosts of delight awake for a shining moment,
And all is troubled, and that desolate land

Remembers grass and flowers, and birds that sang
    there
Their miracles of song in lovely trees,
And waters that poured, or stood, in dreaming
    azure,
Praising the sky. Perhaps once more it sees

The rose, the moon, the pool, in the blue evening,
And knows that silence in which one bird will
    sing
Slowly and sleepily his praise of gardens.
Perhaps once more, for a moment, it remembers
    spring.

                                    Conrad Aiken

INDEXES

INDEX TO AUTHORS

INDEX TO TITLES

INDEX TO FIRST LINES

ACKNOWLEDGMENTS

Thanks are due to the following for permission to include copyrighted poems:

The Atlantic Monthly Company, for "To a Wild Goose over Decoys" by Lew Sarett, Copyright © by The Atlantic Monthly Company, Boston, Mass.

Barrie & Jenkins Publishers and Macmillan Publishing Co., Inc. for "The Mayfly" and "The Coffin-Worm" from *Collected Poems* by Ruth Pitter, Copyright © 1968 by Ruth Pitter.

George Braziller, Inc. for "The Whelk" from *The Pocket Mirror* by Janet Frame, Copyright © 1967 by Janet Frame.

Curtis Brown, Ltd. for "Flying Crooked" from *Collected Poems* by Robert Graves, Copyright © 1939, 1955, 1958, 1961, 1966 by Robert Graves.

Jonathan Cape Ltd. and Mrs. H. M. Davies and Wesleyan University Press for "Till I Went Out" and "Leaves" from *The Complete Poems of W. H. Davies,* Copyright © 1963 by Jonathan Cape, Ltd.

Chatto and Windus Ltd., Mrs. Laura Huxley, and Harper & Row, Publishers, for "The Cicadas," Copyright 1929 by Aldous Huxley, from *The Collected Poetry of Aldous Huxley* (1971), edited by Donald Watt.

Anthony Delius for his "Chameleon."

Andre Deutsch Limited for "Spiders" from *Married/ Singular* by Philip Oakes.

Doubleday & Company, Inc. for "Snake," copyright © 1955 by Theodore Roethke, "The Heron," copyright 1937 by Theodore Roethke and "First Meditation," copyright © 1956 by Atlantic Monthly Company, all from *Collected Poems of Theodore Roethke.*

The New York Times Company for "The Wood Frog" by John Hay, © 1961 by The New York Times Company.

Oxford University Press, Inc., for "Priapus and the Pool, VII" from *Collected Poems, Second Edition* by Conrad Aiken, Copyright © 1970 by Conrad Aiken; and for "Inversnaid" by Gerard Manley Hopkins.

Random House, Inc. for "Crocidiles" from *Chattanooga* by Ishmael Reed, Copyright © 1973 by Ishmael Reed.

The Literary Trustees of Walter de la Mare, and the Society of Authors as their representative for "No Jewel," "A Queen Wasp," and "The Snowflake."